BIBLICAL SURRENDER

BIBLICAL SURRENDER

MICHAEL SUMMERS

heritagehillspress.com

Copyright © 2021 by Michael Summers

Published by Heritage Hills Press, LLC
   PO Box 562
   201 N Race St
   Spring Hill, KS 66083

All rights reserved. No part of this publication may be reproduced, stored in a retrieval system or transmitted in any form by any means, electronic, mechanical, photocopy, recording or otherwise, without the prior permission of the publisher, except as provided for by USA copyright law. Heritage Hills Press is a registered trademark in the United States of America.

First Printing, 2021

Cover design by Heritage Hills Press®

Scripture quotations are from the ESV® Bible (The Holy Bible, English Standard Version®), copyright © 2001 by Crossway, a publishing ministry of Good News Publishers. Used by permission. All rights reserved.

Print Edition ISBN: 978-1-7373327-5-6
Digital Edition ISBN: 978-1-7373327-4-9

CONTENTS

INTRODUCTION viii

1 Astray 1

2 Breaking Point 13

3 The Art of Surrender 24

4 The Turning 34

5 The War On Independence 46

6 A Warning 57

7 Biblical Surrender 65

INTRODUCTION

When I think about the topic of surrender, my mind swirls with thoughts. Perhaps yours does, too. The term initiates a mental flare of pre-loaded illustrations ranging from addiction recovery to white flags and earth-shattering moments of broken wills. Romanticized images of slow-motion ventures down the aisle between wooden pews, sunsets in solace, lifted hands and tears of joy engulf our perspective of surrender in a Biblical context. There are books filled with applications. Some brush across the surface, minting their vague and catchy applications of "let go and let God." Others inspire emotion with infusions of hope for a better life, dreams of a richer purpose, and promises of a deeper achievable happiness. The buffet of spiritual inspiration literature has stretched the topic of surrender so wide and so thin that it has become as Bilbo Baggins described: "like butter scraped over too much bread."

It seems there is no shortage of self-help, self-willed, self-initiated surrender prescriptions decorating the shelves of bookstores near you. In the wake of all this, many are left with unfulfilled expectations and failed attempts to surrender to God. It appears that the topic of surrender is too broad, too overstated, too basic, and almost meaningless.

Yet, I experience something that contradicts this notion. In pastoral ministry, there are constant gaping holes that appear in almost every context that can only be mended with true, Biblical surrender. It weaves its thread into the tapestry of every counseling session. It floats into the sphere of many sermon applications. It emerges in a host of Sunday conversations and late-night phone calls. It crashes upon the serene moments of the Lord's Supper with bread and cup in hand.

Because of this, I am struck with one immense understatement of a thought: surrender is critical. Understanding Biblical surrender is no simple task meant only for the wayward addict or the obstinate train-wreck. Surrender is a foundational concept meant to be something more—something *permanent*. Yet, I am concerned that surrender often is not understood. Even more, it often is not practiced. For something so important, how is it that Christians everywhere still seem to not grasp the true essence of Biblical surrender? Even deeper, why is it that I have not mastered surrender in such a way that I need never return to it again?

These questions are only a sample of the many behind the writing of this book. The ministry experiences I have met combined with deep personal implications have propelled my drive for a true, simple, clear breakdown of surrender for today's Church. If anything, I desire to know more of God's perspective, to be drawn into Scripture, and emerge with something more objective than vague notions of knee-stains and tears. When we really dig, we discover that at the very core of Biblical surrender lies a brilliant discovery illuminating less about me and more about God. And I need that. You need that.

As we journey across the remaining pages, we will not uncover every single stone of individual experiences that surrender can touch. Instead, we will uncover larger stones that disclose clear Biblical truth—something we can take to apply in every experience no matter the nuance. The discovery of true Biblical surrender should be a discovery of hope. Meaning, when we get the corrective lens of Biblical truth resting in our gaze, we will see opportunity that is clear, burdens that can be lifted, mountains that can be overcome, and a God that is powerful enough to accomplish the impossible task of *changing us*. Will you be patient? Will you be vulnerable? Will you be humble? Then please, join me. Let us peel away the layers of ideas and applications to get at the heart of surrender and see afresh this critical and foundational concept for life. For every day.

1

Astray

"All we like sheep have gone astray; we have turned—every one—to his own way; and the Lord has laid on Him the iniquity of us all." Isaiah 53:6

DANGEROUS ADVICE

I remember a car ride from my final year of high school. I was riding with some friends, discussing a mountain of conceivable future opportunities. The car ride was long and the discussion was sincere. We spoke of college choices, career interests, etc. Like most high school seniors, I was interested in a variety of pursuits. Even though I had many ideas and possibilities before me, in the back of my mind, I already knew where God was calling me. I knew God was calling me to a life of Christian service in ministry. That surely made things more complicated. Why should I be limited by that little twinge in my spirit? And, what if I did follow that ambition? What about all the career paths I found interest in? What about what *I wanted*? That discussion in that car ride began to reveal a problem. The problem was that a piece of my heart was feeding a dark notion: that God's calling on my life was oppressive and confining. So, I resisted in that moment. A selfish part of my heart did not love what God was calling me to do.

As we discussed different options on this car ride, I clearly remember the advice of one of the individuals. They said, "You just need to follow your heart." I liked that advice. It sounded good. It sounded fulfilling. If I were to follow my heart, I could pursue doing the things that I loved and the things that interested me most. It was an opportunity for what I perceived to be freedom. In that moment, their advice seemed wise. In fact, everyone in the car agreed it was good. I remember the driver nodding in approval. However, I was ignorant of one dark truth: the instruction to "follow your heart" was the most dangerous advice I have ever been given. Amazingly, it came at a time when I was on the verge of outright defiance. Why was that advice so dangerous? It was because of Scripture's revelation about the human heart:

> *"All we like sheep have gone astray; we have turned—every one—to his own way..."* (Is. 53:6a)

This verse is rather sharp and illuminating. It teaches us that "our own way," the way we want to go when we follow our hearts, takes us "astray." Astray from what? Astray from God's way. To put it bluntly, we have an internal craving for personal independence. Somewhere in our hearts there is a natural desire to live our way instead of God's way. Our hearts like going "astray" because we like being pioneers of our future. Independence is important to us. It appeals to us. That is why commercials will say things like "Have it *your way*." We like our way. And we find most appealing the idea of not needing or depending on anyone else.

You and I are familiar with this. It showed up long ago for us, when we stopped wanting help tying our shoes or getting buckled into our car seats. That mindset just multiplies as we grow older. In high school, we got sick of our parent's plans and wanted to make our own—to do things the way we wanted. When we settled into our first real jobs, we felt the inner resistance against a boss's demands. It is not just a cheeseburger that we want our way, we want a *life path* that is our way. This is natural. This is built in. Everyone wants to be an independent thinker, independently wealthy, the creators of our own destiny. Admittedly, we do not have a natural craving to be dependent. Our ideas about a fulfilling life typically do not include goals of obedience or that really cringy word: submission. It is against our nature. Why is that? The story in Genesis 3 may perhaps give us a clue.

> *"So when the woman saw that the tree was good for food, and that it was a delight to the eyes, and that the tree was to be desired to make one wise, she took of its fruit and ate, and she also gave some to her husband who was with her, and he ate"*
> (Gen. 3:6).

CRAVING INDEPENDENCE

There is something peculiar about what Eve *saw;* that is, what she perceived to be valuable attached to that tree in the Garden of Eden. When we look deeper, we can see that the very thing enticing Eve was independence from God.

She "saw that the tree was good for food." Regardless of God's instruction, Eve found a forbidden *purpose* for the fruit (independence from God's instructed purpose).

She saw "it was a delight to the eyes." Regardless of God's instruction, Eve found a forbidden *pleasure* in the fruit (independence from God's instruction for pleasure).

She saw "that the tree was desired to make one wise." Regardless of God's instruction, Eve found a forbidden *wisdom* to be received from the fruit (independence from God's instruction and wisdom).

You see, it was independence that Satan was after with Eve. Satan wanted God's highest creation on the earth to revolt against the Creator. If this could happen, it would ruin the original purpose of God (all of creation bringing glory and praise to Himself forever). If Satan could trick created beings into seeking their own purpose, it would be his greatest attack against God. We all know the story. Satan's plan worked. After Adam and Eve chose independence, every person has been born with a broken nature—a nature that craves to be independent from God.

You and I can relate to that. Think about a time when you have made a bad choice or did something you knew was wrong. You can probably remember a strong urge to do what you *wanted*. In a past failure, do you remember how powerful that urge was in your heart? You ended up sinning because it was what you *wanted*. Our personal history is living proof that something inside craves independence from God. It shows up when we face the decision to obey or disobey God. The urge screams louder and louder to do exactly what we want—no matter the cost.

So why was the advice to "follow your heart" such bad advice? The answer is simple and blunt. My heart is not safe. If I follow my heart there is something inside that will only lead me (1) away from God's purposes, (2) away from God's pleasures, and (3) away from God's wisdom. This is what the "astray way" is.

THE ASTRAY WAY

Perhaps you agree with most of this so far. You can see that we already have selfish desires within our human nature. That is not too difficult to recognize. Still, there are many people who agree with these things and have this knowledge but continue in a pattern of going astray. This is because, although the knowledge is there, a belief still exists that the "astray way" is not a bad choice. When someone chooses to follow the selfish desires of the heart, they really do not have a problem with the "astray way." In fact, it seems to be the right way—the best way. Scripture has something to say about this:

"There is a way that seems right to a man, but its end is the way to death" (Prov. 16:25).

That is a strong statement. The "astray way" is the way to death? By no means does this verse guarantee that you will be killed instantly for disobeying God. It does not mean you will walk outside and immediately get hit by a truck if you go your own way in life. Rather, it speaks of an eventual ongoing killing. We will see that in a moment. This is not at all referring to a physical death, but a spiritual death. Spiritual death is much different than your heart stopping. It is different than simply an end to your life. The truth is, spiritual death is far worse than physical death.

> *"And do not fear those who kill the body but cannot kill the soul. Rather fear him who can destroy both soul and body in hell"* (Matt. 10:28).

Spiritual death is not an end. It is an ongoing horrific peril that never ends. This is different from our usual concept of death. We often see death as an end to something, not an ongoing experience. However, spiritual death is a very real, unimaginable, constant torment. It is a destroying of both your body and soul that never stops being destroyed. This is hard to comprehend, but this is where the "astray way" leads. It leads to Hell.

There are three major things (among so many others) that make Hell and spiritual death the worst possible experience in all existence.

1. God's grace is not in Hell. All people in this life experience God's "common grace." This is the grace of

God seen in things like health, sunshine and rain, protection, conveniences, opportunities and enjoyment in life. This means that going astray and seeking independence from God finally reaches a horrifying destination. The grace of God that blesses, protects, gives mercy, provides rest, establishes peace and produces joy has been removed. When you finally reach a destination where there is no more common grace, what do you have? You have nothing good left in your existence: no blessing, no protection, no mercy, no rest, no peace, no joy. Why? Because all of those things are experienced only through the grace of God. There is no grace of God in Hell. Amazingly, some people are ok with that. But they do not realize what else is in Hell.

2. Hell is a place of punishment. This is a brand new experience for any human. When a person enters into Hell, for the first time they experience God's wrath and anger. In this terrifying event, one finally comprehends that God is the Supreme Being of the universe, and His wrath and anger are infinitely unbearable. God's punishment is worse than anything that exists in this universe. There is nothing that compares to it. There is fire that burns the body, worms that never stop eating the body while it burns and never one second of relief. There is no relief, because God's grace is not there protecting, giving mercy, giving rest, giving peace. There is no way out. Literally there is no safe place, nowhere to run, and no relief from the pain. That is not all.

3. Hell is a place of total darkness. Never again will the person who enters be able to see again. It's the darkest of all darkness. Simultaneously, in that darkness, one realizes that they are alone. That means no one sees anyone else. No one gets to hang out and chat with buddies who make it there. Instead there is just that awful sound: the sound of the loud screams of others experiencing the same unbearable punishment mixed in with a person's own screaming.

This is where the "astray way" leads. At the end of the path is a drop off into the most unimaginable horror of being constantly destroyed without end. Sadly, many people are running down this path. People are even cheering for the people running down this path! The way of independence may be celebrated, but it is the way to death. So, the advice to "follow your heart" is the most dangerous advice of all. It is the direction that sounds sweet and good and bright but leads to a place where God's grace is removed—a place where His wrath and anger are relentlessly crushing bodies and souls who refused to follow Him. Every human being is born already running down this path.

What about Christians? What about those who do know Jesus, but have struggled and sought to go back to the "astray way"? Here are three things the "astray way" provides for believers.

- It provides *emptiness*. One time a friend showed me a Tootsie Roll flavored chap stick. Because I was trying

BIBLICAL SURRENDER

to be an idiot and funny, I took a bite. I knew it was not a real Tootsie Roll, but it smelled great! I will never forget that awful sensation of wax in my mouth. In a similar way, a believer knows deep in their heart that turning away from God is not going to be satisfying long-term...but it looks so good! The result is that the desire to be happy and the craving to be fulfilled ends up being a letdown. Turning away from real, deep satisfaction in God to pursue lesser satisfaction is like eating chap stick hoping it tastes better than a Tootsie Roll. Everything that seemed to look good ends up tasting like unpleasant wax.

- It provides *loneliness*. I remember the first time I got lost at the store as a kid. As I tagged along near the shopping cart, my eyes became glued to the aisle full of shiny, dazzling toys just waiting to be played with. I took a few steps into the aisle, delighted by the world of fun that lay in my gaze. After a few moments of playing, everything seemed to go dark. I was alone. And the result was a moment of terror. My mom was wisely waiting for me, barely outside of my gaze to teach me a lesson. The "astray way" is like that for a Christian. God has not left or forsaken us. But when we choose independence, it leaves us feeling as if we are lost and separated from God's love and protection. We are unable to feel His presence and we feel utterly alone. This means that peace and security are no longer felt or experienced.
- It provides *misery and regret*. When we reject God, He allows us to run away and experience the emptiness and

loneliness of doing life all by ourselves. The more we seek fulfillment our way, the more miserable we will become. We eventually reach a point where we realize that our time has been wasted and we have failed to fulfill God's intended purpose for our lives. Then comes the heaviness of regret.

Without God, you and I are hopeless beings. We cannot find permanent fulfillment. We cannot always protect ourselves. We cannot meet the deepest needs and desires of our own hearts. We desperately need Him! Can you imagine my 4-year-old telling me that he is a better driver than I am? He cannot reach the pedals! On a grander scale, it is impossible for us to function independently of God and succeed.

Why did we have to go through all of that? The answer is simple: we cannot understand Biblical surrender without first grappling with the human condition and tendencies—and where they lead. We need God's help. If we rush straight into solutions of applying surrender, it only leads to cosmetic adjustment. It is like trying to fix an oil leak in your car by adding more oil. It does not address the problem. I fear that many Christians today try to go about surrendering to God without identifying the true danger that lies within the tendencies of the heart. *How* and *why* you and I got into this position in the first place needs to be properly recognized if there is to be any hope for escaping that condition permanently. In the next few chapters, we will begin to uncover the other side of the story: God's amazing wisdom and power to produce something within us called surrender.

Chapter 1 Study Questions

What is the "astray way"?

Describe the ways that Eve was tempted towards independence.

How does that same temptation for independence reveal itself in your life?

Describe where the "astray way" leads for both unbelievers and believers. Can you explain why?

Why is it dangerous to "follow your heart"?

2

Breaking Point

"The sacrifices of God are a broken spirit; a broken and contrite heart, O God, you will not despise." Psalm 51:17

THE STRUGGLE

Mark had a fantastic family...at least, that is what everyone thought. His family was exciting, active, and always did things together. They had great vacations, made memories, and enjoyed the fruits of his dad's hard work. They were able to drive nice cars and Mark was even able to drive a new car to school and work. To people outside the home, it seemed like Mark had the ideal situation. His parents were generous and loved so many people. They were active in their church and his dad was a great leader for so many other men in the congregation. However, Mark felt differently about his family. People could not see the way his dad treated him when he "messed up" in any area of his life. His dad was not violent, but he was authoritative, voicing his disapproval and providing consequences for inappropriate behavior.

In his heart, Mark felt trapped, almost as if he was not allowed to learn and grow by making mistakes. His parents seemed to expect perfection. Whenever he overstepped boundaries, his parents would take away everything, leaving him feeling childish. Mark began to resent his dad. He saw other people praising his dad and it only angered him more. He became frustrated when his dad would come home from work and start telling him what to do. So, Mark began to stand up to his dad. He began to defy him in front of the family and argue over the smallest things that his dad told him to do. Before long, Mark began to admit that he could not wait to be on his own. He wanted to be free from the tyrant called "dad" that everyone praised and loved. He wanted to be his own man. He wanted to be…independent. To his friends, Mark began to talk about his problems at home. Because of the way he talked about it, others began to think that Mark really needed to be free. After all, he was 18 and almost done with high school. He should be able to make his own decisions and set his own boundaries, right? That is exactly what Mark wanted to hear. He was tired of saying "I have to ask permission from my dad" whenever people wanted to hang out or do anything fun.

Unfortunately, what Mark could not see was that the problem was not with his dad or his family. The problem was in Mark's heart. He was unwilling to love and submit to the authority God had placed in his life. Mark's problem was self-centered pride. That pride showed up in Mark's attitude, in his words, and eventually in his actions. He began to hide things from his parents because he wanted to deal with them by himself. Little did Mark know that he was slowly eroding the greatest relationships on earth: his family.

This is a miniature version of how many Christians function in their relationship with their Creator. God calls believers His "children." As children of God, believers enjoy the benefits of their Heavenly Father's grace. There is limitless love and joy and peace available through that special relationship. However, many Christians get frustrated with God's standards and God's plans. Focusing on all the restrictions and pursuits that God forbids, many Christians begin to feel "trapped" just like Mark. When God has a different plan or brings difficulty, it appears that God is a tyrant, confining, and oppressive.

Looking around at the lives of others does not help. When we see other people enjoying their independence from God, it becomes easier to want that kind of life. The fundamental problem with Mark and many Christians is the same: self-centered pride. Respect for authority dwindles away. Love for authority fades. Joy in the relationship seems like distant history, and what is left is a power-struggle. Submitting to God's authority becomes more difficult and frustrating—even boring. Eventually, there is little desire for the relationship anymore.

THE BIG REVEAL

One day, Mark met with his pastor. As he began to spill out all his feelings through the tears, he felt like he was understood. He had made a great case for his difficult situation and maybe his pastor would even help set his parents straight. They would finally give him the freedom and respect that he felt he needed. The response of Mark's pastor was not what he expected. He said, "Mark, instead of trying to fix all the ways your parents seem to need improvement, you need to understand something more important. You are the problem." That was hard to swallow. As they talked, Mark began to see something he never had before. He began to see that it was not his dad who needed change, but rather it was his own heart. In his heart he despised authority. It had never occurred to Mark that he was valuing himself above others, and that he was seeking only to please and live for himself. What really began to open his eyes was a passage about the obedience of Jesus.

"Have this mind among yourselves, which is yours in Christ Jesus, who, though he was in the form of God, did not count equality with God a thing to be grasped, but emptied himself, by taking the form of a servant, being born in the likeness of men. And being found in human form, he humbled himself by becoming obedient to the point of death, even death on a cross"
(Phil. 2:5-8).

Jesus was obedient. Mark had never really considered the wonder of Jesus' obedience in a situation that was desperate and difficult. Jesus in His humanity struggled with what would take place: His crucifixion and separation from God. But in all this, Jesus obeyed. He obeyed His Father's plan.

Even though He was equal in "God-ness" to the Father, He lived in humble obedience to God the Father.

When Mark realized this, he broke. He understood that his desire to be equal with his dad and be independent was the attitude of Satan, not Jesus. Just like Lucifer desired to be equal with his Authority, Mark had wanted equality with his earthly authority. Just like Adam and Eve had wanted to be equal to God and be independent, Mark had wanted to be equal with his dad and be independent from him. Mark's heart ached as he saw his disgusting rebellion and self-centeredness with clarity. He had been wrong this whole time, with pride distorting his view of his family and his relationship with his dad.

Mark's sin was now gross and shameful to him. But that was not all that troubled Mark. He saw that Jesus died for his rebellion. The pain, agony, and separation from the Father that Jesus experienced on the cross was to pay the price for who Mark had been. Oh, how we need to be at that same place as Mark! We must see that we can never be equal with our Heavenly Authority. Instead, we are nothing more than tiny creations—even our own abilities to succeed physically and spiritually are worthless. When we crave to go the "astray way," we are in essence craving to be equal with God as the authority and master of our lives. To put it plainly, it is a power struggle. Jesus paid a terrible price for the wickedness of this selfish kind of revolt against God. While our hearts have been so occupied with having life our way, we have been heaping agony upon agony on the heart, soul, and body of the Savior at the cross.

APPROACHING THE PROBLEM

How do we get on board with God's plan? How do we get on the path of dependence instead of independence? This is where many people mistakenly slip back into the "astray way." Here are a couple incorrect approaches:

1. *The "self-made" approach.* This is a common one. People who take this approach start adding in all kinds of really good things. It comesced out in ways such as "I need to do more devotions." "I need to volunteer in more ministries." "I just need to go to church more." They start trying to do things for God. Those are all great things. In fact, those are things that can propel a relationship with God (when approached on different terms). Unfortunately, those who take the "self-made" approach find themselves getting burned out. After a few weeks it becomes too difficult to spend time in God's Word, volunteering becomes a burden, and life gets too crazy to make it to church consistently. When these things break down, the fight against sin feels more like trying to lift an elephant with bare hands. No one succeeds in the "self-made" approach to try harder and do better for God. The result is that people give up because they see the impossibility of success. The enemy wins again.

2. *The "super-protective" approach.* This is also a common one. Those who take this approach completely rearrange life through extreme measures. They change their schedules, throw away their televisions, and get rid

BIBLICAL SURRENDER

of all the items they own that took time away from God or tempted them towards sin. This approach looks very admirable. They literally eliminate everything in their lives that they think pulled them away from God. Over time, all those protections start to seem unnecessary. They start to get weary of all the "inconveniences" of their radically structured life. They start feeling the regrets of getting rid of that 85" television. Eventually, it gets too hard to be so overprotective, and all the barriers slowly break down. With a sigh, they hop right back on the "astray way." Score another point for the enemy.

Why do those approaches always fail? Is there something wrong with doing more devotions, "doing more church," and setting up stricter standards in life? No...unless those things are the first response. The reason is that every single one of those things are external. They might seem like great things to do on the outside, but the most important part is missing. It is like telling a man who is having a heart attack to stop eating fried chicken. That is a good idea, but it does not address the emergency within. (By the way, yes, you do need more devotions!)

The Psalmist points us to the kind of response that is appropriate:

"For you will not delight in sacrifice, or I would give it; you will not be pleased with a burnt offering. The sacrifices of God are a broken spirit; a broken and contrite heart, O God, you will not despise" (Ps. 51:16-17).

This is exactly what God desires in us. God is not pleased by a bunch of good religious "things" as our response to Him. What delights God, and is the first step to getting on the path of dependence, is a broken heart. Those who have a broken heart are severely convicted by their sin. When they come to the realization of how big God is and how small they are in comparison, things get scary. In this moment, the ugly, self-centered pride that has ruled their life is now seen with clear vision. The result is horrifying. They are able to see that their pride has really been a revolt against the Almighty God, because they have been living as their own god. They have been trying to seize control of the throne of their heart.

For true believers, God is already on that throne. He must be recognized as the King. That is why one can do all kinds of great and godly things to get on the right path, but always fail. When a person ignores God's rule, they will fail to turn their life around every single time. The only way to approach God and get on the path of dependence is to approach Him as the rightful King of your heart.

For those who are not true believers, there is a different problem. God is not on the throne in their heart. There is another: self. That ruler does not hold enough power for change, and in the deepest way wants to retain control of that throne. That ruler needs to be dethroned. If that is you, and if you are at a place in life where you finally recognize your need for a better King, your life is on the cusp of a most glorious revolution. You are finally in the right place to surrender. In our next chapter we will begin to discover how this surrender takes place.

Chapter 2 Study Questions

Describe Mark's "problem" and how he responded.

Describe Jesus' response to the authority of God the Father. How was that example used in Mark's life?

List some unsuccessful approaches to surrender and explain why those do not work.

What are some ways you have sought control of the throne of your heart?

Why does God delight in a broken, contrite heart?

3

The Art of Surrender

"For by the grace given to me I say to everyone among you not to think of himself more highly than he ought to think, but to think with sober judgment, each according to the measure of faith that God has assigned." Romans 12:3

BATTLE WORDS

The English word "surrender" is a word that has been used in wartime particularly in the last several hundred years. It is always a last resort. Most often, if a particular group of people are losing severely in battle, they either retreat and try to escape or they die fighting. Surrender is rather rare. It usually takes place at the very end of a war, bringing about peace and an end to all fighting. In the American Civil War, there were a series of surrenders over the course of seven months that marked the end of the majority of war activity. General Robert E. Lee surrendered to General Ulysses S. Grant on April 9, 1865. Over the next seven months, there were 38 surrenders of various Confederate troops, the final of which took place on November 6, 1865. What exactly took place in those surrenders? For most, a document was signed by the surrendering party signifying that they would no longer fight and would be at the mercy of the winning side.

General Lee's surrender on April 9, 1865 included a series of terms or conditions. General Lee stated that he would surrender if certain requests were granted and promises were made. General Grant agreed, and what followed was known as a "conditional surrender." Within the terms of that surrender, all the surrendering officers were allowed to keep their swords and side arms. The soldiers could keep their horses and mules in order to return home and use them in the upcoming season of planting and farming. Therefore, it was a "conditional surrender."

At the end of World War II, the Germans were given an order of "unconditional surrender." This was much different than General Lee's option in the American Civil War. The Germans would not receive any promises, exceptions or benefits other than what was declared under the international laws of war. They had to give up all weapons, all resources, and keep nothing. Everything they had they were required to give up to the Allied nations.

SURRENDER COMMANDED

Spiritually, there is a war in our own hearts. In this war we are called to an unconditional surrender. That means no special exceptions or special allowances. It is to be a surrender that is complete, holding nothing back. Jesus describes this surrender so well in Luke 9.

"To another he said, 'Follow me.' But he said, 'Lord, let me first go and bury my father.' And Jesus said to him, 'Leave the dead to bury their own dead. But as for you, go and proclaim the kingdom of God.' Yet another said, 'I will follow you, Lord, but let me first say farewell to those at my home.' Jesus said to him, 'No one who puts his hand to the plow and looks back is fit for the kingdom of God'" (Luke 9:59-62).

The terms for surrender to God are unconditional. We are to leave everything in life behind. Jesus is not teaching that we are to forsake our families and cut all communications with our loved ones. Rather, Jesus is teaching that to surrender to God and be on the path of dependence, we cannot hold on to anything—no matter the value—if it makes us resistant to Him. There is to be nothing that we can still claim as our own. There is to be nothing that we still value and cherish more than following Jesus. We are to literally give up our claim to everything in our lives. It means God owns us, our bodies, souls, relationships, and futures. One cannot fully surrender to God while still pursuing some other dream or ambition. Jesus requires it all. Why? Because anything that we still hold on to or pursue or cherish to keep for ourselves leaves room for future insubordination. That is what makes surrender difficult. It is a total and complete giving up of all that we are, all that we have, and all that we desire.

> *"No servant can serve two masters, for either he will hate the one and love the other, or he will be devoted to the one and despise the other. You cannot serve God and money"* (Luke 16:13).

SURRENDER AS A GIFT

Surrender does not begin with us making a decision. It actually starts before any of our actions or decisions take place. It is first a gift from God.

> *"For by the grace given to me I say to everyone among you not to think of himself more highly than he ought to think, but to think with sober judgment, each according to the measure of faith that God has assigned"* (Rom. 12:3).

Surrender begins with faith that is given from God: "faith that God has assigned." It is not something that you and I can just go out there and "do" when we feel like it. God's work in salvation proves this.

> *"For by grace you have been saved through faith. And this is not your own doing; it is the gift of God"* (Eph. 2:8).

Faith that is in us, moving us to surrender, is graciously gifted to us by God. That is why we cannot claim salvation as our own doing. If we could create our own faith, we would be able to claim it was our ability and wisdom that turned our hearts toward embracing salvation. We would not need God's help to have saving faith—the faith to surrender. It would mean that we could still be our own gods on the throne of our hearts. Real faith leading to surrender only comes from God.

SURRENDER AS AN ART

Talking about surrender as an art may at first give you the wrong impression. When phrased that way, we easily think of ourselves in the place of a craftsman or artist. In reality, the opposite is true. Surrender is an art, but it is not our artwork. It is not our craft. It is the perfect artwork of the Perfect Craftsman. Not only is God the one who grants faith to us, but He is the one who grows our faith and moves our faith to the place of surrender. It is something that God is at work in the heart of a believer to perfect over a lifetime.

> *"...let us run with endurance the race that is set before us, looking to Jesus, the founder and perfecter of our faith..."* (Heb. 12:1b-2a).

He begins with conviction of sin. The one who begins to experience God convicting them of their sin and wickedness is the one whom God is beckoning. He is carefully alerting their conscience. At this point many people make a choice to ignore God's beckoning and convicting work. This is called rebellion. Rebellion is a disgusting eruption of pride at the slightest feeling of God's touch. If we do not resist God's work of conviction, however, we begin to feel the weight of guilt. When you and I experience conviction over sin and the heaviness of guilt, we must not think we are being punished. Guilt and conviction are not punishments, but rather are beautiful, gracious works of God in our hearts.

God uses conviction and guilt to move us to confession. He uses those pressures to initiate within us our first response of confessing our sin. This is the low point. This is the place where we admit to God our ugliness and the cold disobedience of our hearts. However, this is not the finished product. Confessing does not fix the problem. You and I know this all too well. We are familiar with confessing a sin only to return to it again and again. Confession is great in that it recognizes and agrees with God's verdict of "guilty." God is at work to do more than that.

As we confess our sins to the Lord and finally see a clear picture, we feel a deep sense of grief. Grief happens when we are convicted, feel the shame and guilt of our sin, confess our sin to God, and finally see our situation with clarity. Paul's response in Scripture erupts in:

> *"Wretched man that I am! Who will deliver me from this body of death?"* (Rom. 7:24)

Grief is purposeful. When we grieve over sin, we mourn. This is only supposed to last a short time. Unfortunately, even at this point, many people again resist God's craftsmanship and choose to stay at the grief stage. Instead of moving ahead, the grieving stage turns into an ugly pile of self-focus and prideful pity. When this happens, it is as if one says, "Stop the train, God. I am not going any further. I want to stay here."

That itself is a trap. The trap is pride and self-pity that resists obedience and instead puts all the attention on how I *feel* about what I have done. Many people choose to stay at the grief stage and swim in the pool of feelings. At the extreme, some even feel the need to grieve as a way of paying for their sins. This is not the Gospel. The Gospel in no way gives us the right or responsibility to pay for sins with guilt. Jesus paid it all. Grief is to serve a different purpose.

God moves us to grief only so that we can have the motivation to repent. That means the feelings we experience in grief are designed to push us to something further and greater.

> *"For godly grief produces a repentance that leads to salvation without regret, whereas worldly grief produces death"* (2 Cor. 7:10).

Grief is like fuel that burns in our hearts propelling us to run away from our sin and wickedness. Therefore, those who find it difficult to repent of sin and turn away from the "astray way" sometimes lack the deep motivation of weighted grief. Or, perhaps they have found a way to push away grief through numbness and distraction.

When someone responds in repentance, it is only after God has done the work of convicting, bringing guilt, moving to confession, and producing God-centered grief. This repentance is a turning away completely from sin and running the opposite direction. Repentance is the work of faith that God has done. That means repentance is never separated from faith. It is always the work of faith. God is the One Who convicts, leads us to confession and instills grief—using it to guide us to repentance. This entire process is beautifully constructed and carried out by God. This is the work of the Perfect Craftsman. This is the art of surrender.

Chapter 3 Study Questions

What kind of surrender does God command and why?

Where and how does surrender begin?

Describe God's process of drawing us to surrender.

List some incorrect responses to God's inner working that hinder us from surrendering to Him.

How should faith and repentance work together to set the stage for surrender?

4

The Turning

"All mine are yours, and yours are mine, and I am glorified in them." John 17:10

UNDERSTANDING REPENTANCE

In our last chapter we saw the process God brings us through to initiate repentance, and it is amazing. His work is intricate and beautiful, driving us to that place. This raises a question for us: how can we understand what true repentance is once we get there? That is the question we will explore in this chapter.

Repentance is a concept that saturates the Old and New Testaments. In the days of the prophets in the Old, the nations of Israel and Judah were repeatedly called to repentance. This was because of their rebellion against God and indulgence in pagan worship. The call to repentance, in the most basic sense, was a call to do three things: 1) stop worshipping false gods, 2) start worshipping the true God, and 3) remain dedicated only to the true God. In this we see a stopping, a starting, and a continuation.

In the New Testament, the theme of repentance continues with John the Baptist. Heralded as the prophet who prepared the way for Jesus, John's message of repentance followed a similar formula to that of the Old Testament prophets. 1) His call was for people to stop living for themselves, and 2) to turn to Jesus by faith. Summed up, his message was "repent and believe." The basic concepts of stopping, starting, and continuing are present again.

Jesus furthered the message of repentance in His ministry. In His own words, we can clearly see a similar formula to the repentance described in earlier Scriptures.

> *"The time is fulfilled, and the kingdom of God is at hand; repent and believe in the gospel"* (Mark 1:15).

There is a call to repent and believe, mirroring the formula of stopping, starting, and continuing. However, the marriage of repentance and faith in Jesus' and in John's messages cannot be ignored. That is because the natural progression of true repentance is faith, while at the same time, true repentance begins with faith. This brings some clarity to repentance. It shows us that repentance involves faith from the very beginning, but it also drives faith to continual action.

INCREDIBLE RESULTS

The word "repentance" in the Bible is used two different

ways. One word, the one used in the Old Testament, denotes a change of mind. It has to do with the intellect of a person and a conscious decision by that intellect. In the formula of all three examples we saw in Scripture, this can be described as the "stopping." In relation to our last chapter, this is the result of conviction. God works in the mind of a person to realize they are on the "astray way," and to have the conviction that the outcome will be disastrous. But this is not the completion of repentance. Merely stopping your direction does not give you the freedom that complete repentance provides. There is something more.

The second word used in Scripture, the one Jesus uses, speaks about the emotional side of a person. It is the arresting of the heart. When a person is emotionally moved by their intellectual conviction, it leads to action. This can be described as the "starting." This is because true repentance involves the mind (intellect) and the heart (emotions). The combination of that is a powerful change of direction to do something new: submit to God.

This kind of submission to God is not a one-time event. It places an individual on a different path with a new Ruler, a new direction, and a new purpose. If the astray way is all about a person's own desires and independence, then this new path is the opposite. It is all about Someone else's desires. If the mind and the heart are driven by faith in this other Person (God), then the result is a continual trajectory of life towards knowing Him. I love what Paul says:

> *"...God may perhaps grant them repentance leading to a knowledge of the truth"* (2 Tim. 2:25).

There is a unique result of repentance in that it leads to *knowing*. This knowing or knowledge is not merely intellectual. It is relational. There is a unique "knowing" of God that one experiences through repentance. I love this. God does not uniquely bring a person through the process of repentance only to stay at a distance. Instead, it is through repentance that one finally experiences a true relationship with the One they are repenting *unto*—the One they are turning *toward*. Paul gives a personal example:

> *"I have been crucified with Christ. It is no longer I who live, but Christ who lives in me. And the life I now live in the flesh I live by faith in the Son of God, who loved me and gave himself for me"* (Gal. 2:20).

Paul's example points us directly to Christ and the Gospel. All of the work that God accomplishes in us is because of the Gospel. It is about the Gospel. It is through the Gospel. The Gospel is the truth of Christ's ultimate payment for sin and gift of restoring us to relationship with the Father.

Through Adam and Eve, we all begin life running the "astray way." It is built in, but at the same time chosen by us. It is a bondage that brings with it an impossible debt. The only way for us to pay that debt is to be destroyed for a literal eternity in Hell as we saw in Chapter 1. What Jesus did was shatter the chains of our bondage to this path of sin and death by physically, emotionally, and spiritually paying the debt on our behalf. When He paid that debt, He traded to us His "debtless" account of righteousness before the Father. This is the miracle of the Gospel. That is why Paul says, "I have been crucified with Christ." He is stating that all of his sin and his debt was nailed to Christ Jesus on the cross. Because of that, the perfect and holy standing Jesus had before the Father is now Paul's and ours. This is the beginning of new life. This is the foundation of the new way—the opposite of the "astray way."

Paul illustrates what this is like. He says, "It is no longer I who live." That means that somewhere along the line there is a moment where we respond by completely denying ourselves and then giving up everything to Jesus. It is at this moment that a person transfers all value to Jesus, all command to Jesus, all purpose to Jesus and all desires to Jesus.

AN EXAMPLE

That is exactly what happened in Ashley's life. As a new mom, she had begun to realize the life she always wanted was slipping away. Her dreams of traveling the world were gone. Her career as a physical therapist came to a sudden stop. She had a new baby and was stuck at home. Her husband was gone at work all week. Her friends were all happily making money, buying houses and driving nice cars. While Ashley loved her baby, she hated the way her life had turned out. Because she was so unhappy, she started to try to get some of that happiness back. Ashley felt that she had no value as a stay-at-home mom, so she started blogging.

What Ashley really wanted was to feel valuable. She set up some social media accounts to interact with her blog. She began to provide instruction on topics like raising kids, fitness, gardening, shopping, DIY projects and decorating trends. Her social media accounts were loaded with pictures perfectly edited and worthy of a magazine. After a couple years Ashley had a few thousand people following her online and commenting on her thoughtful tips. Ashley was driven. Even though her efforts were successful, she was not as happy inside her home as she had hoped. While her pictures looked stunning and her tips were far-reaching, her marriage struggled. It was difficult to respond to her husband when there was so much that she was trying to accomplish. His leadership and direction in the home sometimes conflicted with Ashley's goals. He was getting in the way. It became apparent that Ashley's life was all about Ashley.

It was not until a friend from church gently confronted her that Ashley realized what had happened. Her blog and social media accounts were not a sin by themselves, but her heart's desire and motivations were sinful. She had used her family and her home not as a platform to serve and love, but to promote herself. Her husband was lonely and distant. Her little girl was selfish and hateful. Ashley had made everyone slaves to her campaign of being important and trained her daughter to be just like her. So, she sought counseling. As she heard the Gospel, Ashley experienced God's convicting work in her heart moving her to confession and grief over her selfish pride, and ultimately to repentance in her heart. When all this hit her, she got down on her knees and cried out to Jesus. "God, I need You. I have been living completely for myself. I just wanted to be important and valuable and have attention. I have used my family selfishly to serve me instead of giving myself to them. In all of this, God, I have rejected You. I have refused to live for You. God, please take away my selfish desires and give me desires to live for You. I give You all my ambition, all my thoughts, all my feelings and my will. Please use me to do and be exactly what You want—not what I have wanted. I hold nothing back. I am Yours."

In that office on her knees Ashley surrendered. The surrender was a beautiful work of God in her heart and it completely changed her life. That was not just a good spiritual thing for Ashley to do. It was obedience to a command from Scripture.

"I appeal to you therefore, brothers, by the mercies of God, to present your bodies as a living sacrifice, holy and acceptable to God, which is your spiritual worship" (Rom. 12:1).

Surrender is literally a "gifting" of ourselves to God. This is produced as the final step in repentance. When you and I are driven to that step of surrender, there is a very real moment of giving back to God every part of our lives that we have been hoarding for our pleasure and desire. It means giving God the spot on the throne of our hearts. This puts us in a place of owning nothing about ourselves. No more living for self. No more attempting to live life for the sole purpose of bringing ourselves pleasure. This is unconditional surrender. Life now moves forward with the sole purpose of doing and being what God has designed us to do and be. And the best place for this step to take place is in private prayer just like Ashley did.

KEEP ON GIVING

The uniqueness of this step is that it keeps on stepping. Surrender is continual. It is to be an action of permanence, meaning it must drive us toward God and away from ourselves permanently. Paul uses the term "living sacrifice" in Romans 12:1. Sacrifice was a very important word to the people of Israel. It was a real action that was a part of their culture and religious system. But never in the history of sacrifice was there a "living sacrifice." All sacrifices died. They were animals that were killed with their blood spilling all over an altar as a payment in exchange for sin. It was final. Every single sacrifice was given and then complete. From the moment the sacrifice ended it was a thing of the past.

This new description of sacrifice is different. Instead of referring to an animal, this command of sacrifice refers to us—our lives. "Living sacrifice" is a sacrifice that stays alive. It remains a sacrifice. What does that mean? That means our life moving forward should not be *for us*. It should be lived for God. Paul speaks of this way of life as being both an inside and outside job. Rather than changing everything on the outside first, change begins within. He says it this way, "It is no longer I who live, but Christ who lives in me" (Gal. 2:20). Christ lives in me; this is internal. The direction we begin to go in surrender to Jesus is a direction that is totally ruled by Him, not ruled by us.

When I speak of the internal part of a person, I am referring to their mind, their emotions, and their will. These are the parts of us that feel, think, desire, and make decisions. Each of them, when ruled and driven by Jesus, produce different ways of thinking, feeling, wanting, and choosing than what we are used to. What is different is that each of them belongs to Jesus and depends on Jesus. This is only possible, as we have seen, through the faith that is gifted to us by God. When our inner beings (mind, desires, emotions and will) belong to Jesus and depend on Him, our lives seek something different. We begin seeking to obey and bring glory to God. The effect of this inside change is that the way our lives function on the outside takes a new direction. When our minds, emotions and wills belong to God and are driven by a new desire to bring Him glory, it also affects the way we speak, act and use our bodies.

This the same way an apple tree works. When an apple seed is planted (under the right circumstances), it takes root and sprouts into a small green plant. Over time the plant grows, and bark is formed. Leaves grow as the plant gets taller and taller. Eventually, the plant is a full-grown tree with roots, a trunk, branches, leaves and apples. It would be silly to try to turn an apple tree into an orange tree. If you picked off all the apples and then used duct tape to put oranges all over the tree, it still would not be an orange tree. That is because the tree itself all the way down to the roots is still an apple tree.

Change is like this in our lives. We cannot use spiritual

duct tape to try and make our lives look like Jesus. We need change down at the root level. It is the change at the roots of our hearts that produce Jesus-like lives on the outside. We must surrender at the very roots. All of this is to be a continual process for the believer. Surrender is a way of life, not a one-time event. As we *live a surrendered life*, God shows us His purposes, gives us new desires, and makes us into a new kind of people that live differently.

Being a living sacrifice is the way we can best worship God. Paul states that in Romans 12:1. He says, "this is your spiritual worship." The question we are faced with at the end of this chapter is this: "have I surrendered everything at the roots?" If the answer is "no," what is it that you are holding on to that you cannot let yourself give away to God? Real surrender is unconditional. There is nothing we are to hold back. There is to be nothing left for us to still keep and pursue for ourselves. When we surrender, all our pursuits of pleasure, happiness and fulfillment now belong to God. If you cannot respond to God in this way, you are still on the path of independence. You are choosing the path called "the astray way."

Chapter 4 Study Questions

How does the Gospel relate to Biblical surrender?

In what ways did Ashley's choices and mindset affect everything else in her life?

What are some key things about surrender that you observed in Ashley's prayer?

How does Romans 12:1 clarify God's expectation of surrender?

Explain the truth pictured by the apple tree illustration.

5

The War On Independence

"Search me, O God, and know my heart! Try me and know my thoughts! And see if there be any grievous way in me, and lead me in the way everlasting!" Psalm 139:23-24

WHAT NOW?

We still have not seen the complete results of surrender. I trust that thus far you have been able to understand just how intricately God is involved in producing this kind of faith and how to respond in that faith. At this point, I am delighted to share with you the results. There is something that God produces in us as we surrender: unspeakable joy.

"You make known to me the path of life; in your presence there is fullness of joy; at your right hand are pleasures forevermore" (Psalm 16:11).

Joy is a gracious blessing of God that is found in abun-

BIBLICAL SURRENDER

dance when we surrender to Him. This is because surrender helps us to stop resisting God as He draws us closer to Himself. As the Psalmist said, the fullness of joy is found in the presence of God. It is finally here at this place of closeness to God that we experience a joy like no other. It is a precious, deep, satisfying joy that is richer than any pleasure we get on the "astray way." Isn't that amazing? When we finally stop seeking our own pleasure and give ourselves to God for His pleasure, what we actually find is better pleasure than we have ever experienced! That is a huge encouragement for us. God did not have to bless us in this way, but by His rich, abundant grace we experience a new joy in the freedom of surrender. This satisfies our souls and fuels us to continue as living sacrifices.

Let me illustrate how this works. Since true surrender holds nothing back, it gives away to God every part of the heart. Among those things given to God are the desires of the heart. When our sinful desires are given to God, He gives us holy and pure desires that crave Him.

> *"Delight yourself in the Lord, and He will give you the desires of your heart"* (Psalm 37:4).

These new desires from God are good cravings. With new desires to live for God, we are fueled to seek God passionately. Here is the great part: God does not run away. We find Him. How do we find Him? We hear Him speak to us through His Word. We feel His Spirit at work in us convicting, guiding, comforting, giving peace, infusing strength and hope. When we find God in this way, we experience the purest fulfillment of our new God-given desires. Think about this. Instead of seeking pleasure that may never be found, through surrender God gives us deep desires that He fulfills in our hearts again and again. This causes us to echo with the Psalmist:

"Oh, taste and see that the LORD is good!" (Ps. 34:8a)

Can you imagine having desires that God loves and at the same time feeling the joy and satisfaction of those desires being met by God? This is one of the many extraordinary blessings that come from following Jesus. This joy does not only serve a purpose of pleasure; it serves as a weapon. Joy helps to fight a very real and dark battle in our hearts.

HELP NEEDED

Unfortunately, the moment of surrender can be short-lived. I have heard people describe this as "coming off the top of a mountain only to descend into the deepest valley." After the new feelings of joy and freedom fade, we can start to feel something old creeping back into our hearts: the urge to be independent. If left unchecked, we can easily go back to the familiar urges in our hearts and begin to obey them. This is the war waging inside every believer. We will refer to it as "the war on independence." This is a common war that was waged even in the heart of Paul.

"So I find it to be a law that when I want to do right, evil

lies close at hand. For I delight in the law of God, in my inner being, but I see in my members another law waging war against the law of my mind and making me captive to the law of sin that dwells in my members" (Rom. 7:21-23).

Here is what Paul is referring to. For believers, there are two different kinds of desires in our hearts: old desires for independence and new, pure desires from God. These are both at odds and create conflict within. They are what keep our hearts from being completely trustworthy. Like the danger in the advice I received in Chapter 1 to follow my heart, it is not safe to just do what I feel. I cannot trust my heart completely, because there are dangerous urges inside. The good news is that there is a way to fight against the urge to be independent. In a basic way, we are to fight independence with dependence. The book of Psalms is loaded with expressions of dependence and humility. One in particular stands out as a weapon:

"Search me, O God, and know my heart! Try me and know my thoughts! And see if there be any grievous way in me, and lead me in the way everlasting!" (Ps. 139:23-24)

In order to fight against the independence of our hearts we need help. That is why the first cry of the Psalmist we just read recognized God's power and authority. It is God's power and God's authority that demand our allegiance and our dependence. The problem we face in our "independence cravings" is a problem of self-worth and self-ability. In a way, we can gradually think of ourselves as equal with God. When this happens we believe that somehow we have the ability and wisdom to guide ourselves to lasting pleasure apart from God's help. That is incredibly dangerous, but many Christians live this way. The truth is, we will never be dependent on God if we believe that we are equal with Him.

How does this show up? It shows up in our behavior (seeking our own way), in our attitudes (feeling like we can handle life), and in our communication (promoting our abilities and wisdom). The Psalmist had a different approach. He begins by asking God for help. He cries out to God about something very personal: his heart, admitting that he needs help on the inside. This shows us that the battle against independence must be faced head-on in the heart. In our hearts we face the temptation to turn back to the "astray way"—the way of independence. Recognizing this internal warfare, the Psalmist pleads for God to search his heart. That means he is asking God to find any place where he has drifted back toward independence. There is a goal in mind. He is not just asking God to point out error, he is asking God to lead him in the way he should go.

At the bottom line of all of this is *dependence*. This must be our goal. There is a sense in which some Christians stop half-way. Rather than seeking to depend on God and follow His leading, they simply want God to help point out a few errors. That is like saying, "Hey, God, please show me where I am messing up. Ok, thanks for that, I've got it from here." We must not approach God that way. We need more than God's observation; we need His guidance! When we seek God's help, we must seek it with an eager heart to follow Him in obedience.

REPAIR REQUIRED

One of the many ways that God guides us and shows us how to obey is through His Word. How do you view the Bible? Do you see it as dry sand to sift through, or do you see it as a well of pure water that can quench your greatest thirst? Your view of God's Word will determine how you approach it. In the war on independence, God's Word is of the highest importance for us. We can see that through Paul's instruction immediately following the command to be "living sacrifices."

> *"Do not be conformed to this world, but be transformed by the renewal of your mind, that by testing you may discern what is the will of God, what is good and acceptable and perfect"* (Rom. 12:2).

To keep from going back to the "astray way" (conforming to this world), Paul says to be "transformed by the renewal of your mind" (Rom. 12:2). What does that mean? Am I supposed to just go out there and try to keep my mind in healthy spiritual shape? No. Being renewed in our minds is not about us fixing ourselves, but instead going into the Divine Workshop where God operates on us through His Word.

> *"But that is not the way you learned Christ!—assuming that you have heard about him and were taught in him, as the*

truth is in Jesus, to put off your old self, which belongs to your former manner of life and is corrupt through deceitful desires, and to be renewed in the spirit of your minds" (Eph. 4:20- 23).

"Be renewed in the spirit of your minds." Not only do our hearts need help, but our minds need transformation. To be specific, there are things within our minds that need to be fixed. The part that needs fixing is the constant mindset you and I fall back into—a mind that places self at the center of life, exalting and lifting self to the position of being king. How do we renew that mind? It is renewed by constantly feasting on God's Word. As we feast, we are reminded of our place as servants of the great King Jesus. We are reminded of the Gospel. God uses His Word to return us to the perspective we had at the cross. Ultimately, God uses His Word to accomplish in us the work of conviction, guilt, confession, grief, repentance, and surrender.

This is exactly what we need. When renewed, our minds can think clearly as children of God, not slaves to our former cravings. I have heard some Christians say that they do not need to read God's Word because they "already understand and know what His Word says." They no longer see a need to constantly feast on Scripture. That is so dangerous! How are we to be confronted with the right perspective if we refuse to have our minds renewed in Scripture?

My brother's truck reminds me of this. When he went off to college, I drove his blue 1988 Chevy Silverado for over a year. I knew that the engine needed oil, but I did not want to take the time to go to the local shop to get an oil change. I decided that I would just throw in a little oil every few months. I thought I knew better. What I did not realize was that the old oil turned to a dirt-filled slime and was beginning to destroy the engine. Finally, the truck died; I had murdered the engine. I should have taken it to a shop to get the oil renewed on a regular basis. If I had done that, the old oil would have been purged and the new oil would have been able to do its proper work.

It works the same way with Scripture. We must go to the Divine Workshop to have our minds renewed regularly in God's Word. If we refuse to do this, our thinking slowly gets polluted. Eventually, our polluted thinking causes us to stop depending on God and our lives become consumed with sinful pride. This kills surrender. It causes us to back-track and seek the path of independence. This spiritual war is real. It threatens to cut off our allegiance to God. It threatens to put a stop to our lives being living sacrifices. We must seek God's help rooting out our sin, we must seek wisdom through His Word to renew our minds, and we must seek His guidance and strength for obedience.

So, where are you? Have you been refusing to seek God's help identifying your sin? Have you neglected to seek God's leading away from self-centered perspectives, desires, and habits? Is your thinking polluted because you have ignored the need to have your mind renewed? If so, please do not continue responding with a cry for independence. Will you stop right now and humbly plead with God as the Psalmist did?

"Search me, O God, and know my heart! Try me and know

my thoughts! And see if there be any grievous way in me, and lead me in the way everlasting!" (Ps. 139:23-24)

Enlist in the war on independence by seeking God's help and guidance. Be ready to obey. The war is ferocious, but winning is something our great King specializes in. He can have victory in your heart and in your mind. If you are in the middle of that battle, do not grow weary. Remember, on the other side of surrender is a joy and pleasure too deep for words to describe.

Chapter 5 Study Questions

Describe the way God blesses us following surrender. How does that aid us in the war on independence?

Describe the internal war of a believer. Where is the main battleground for independence/dependence?

List some some ways that your heart is drawn back toward independence.

How does the Psalmist show us an example of surrendered thinking? What are some key elements in seeking dependence on the Lord?

Describe the dangers of neglecting the Word of God. How can you forsake God even when you are filled with a knowledge of His Word?

6

A Warning

"I tell you, this man went down to his house justified, rather than the other. For everyone who exalts himself will be humbled, but the one who humbles himself will be exalted." Luke 18:14

FAKE OUT

The Hague Convention of 1907 specifically states, "It is especially forbidden to make improper use of a flag of truce." In other words, you cannot fake surrender. This was a dirty tactic that had been used in many instances throughout history. It would happen when a particular war party signaled a "truce." As soon as the enemy approached and became vulnerable, they would attack and kill them. Their intention was never to surrender, but instead to trick the other party into believing they surrendered so that they could gain an upper hand for victory.

At our current phase in history, false surrender is prohibited by the international laws of war. Interestingly, earthly war is not the only place that false surrender happens. We also see something about it in Scripture: a spiritual warning.

> *"He also told this parable to some who trusted in themselves that they were righteous, and treated others with contempt: 'Two men went up into the temple to pray, one a Pharisee and the other a tax collector. The Pharisee, standing by himself, prayed thus: 'God, I thank you that I am not like other men, extortioners, unjust, adulterers, or even like this tax collector. I fast twice a week; I give tithes of all that I get.' But the tax collector, standing far off, would not even lift up his eyes to heaven, but beat his breast, saying, 'God, be merciful to me, a sinner!' I tell you, this man went down to his house justified, rather than the other. For everyone who exalts himself will be humbled, but the one who humbles himself will be exalted"*
> (Luke 18:9-14).

Jesus gives an amazing story of two men praying. Both appeared to be in "surrender" to God. Although the first one was very clean on the outside, he had no intention of living for God internally. It may have looked like that to others, but it was a fake surrender. His speech shows us exactly what condition his heart was in. What this man had was a heart consumed with selfish pride. His heart was not broken. He was not humble. In all this he wanted to please himself by trying to look better than everyone else. If he looked better than everyone, people would think the highest of him, and perhaps even God would think well of him. It was a selfish mindset.

BIBLICAL SURRENDER

Ultimately, it meant that he never really surrendered in his heart. The second man, on the other hand, was in the midst of true surrender. He was going through the process of conviction, guilt, confession, grief, and repentance.

I want us to focus on the first man. Everything he did seemed to be evidence of surrender on the outside. Look at how he appears to be on fire for God. He fasts twice a week for God? Wow, he must really have a great prayer life. He tithes consistently from everything he gets paid? Wow, he must really trust God with his finances. Do you see how easy it would be for us to think that this guy is the real deal? It would be very easy. On the inside, however, he had no intention of being broken and humble. His heart's intention was to bring himself pleasure by getting everyone—including God—to think highly of him. Really, he only cared about himself. That is fake surrender.

Fake surrender is giving up to God things in your life so you look better. What that means is that you do not end up surrendering what is on the inside. You only surrender what people can see, but at the same time live as if you were the ruler on the throne of your own heart. Beware of this. Half surrender does not bring you the pleasure that you might think. It cuts you off from getting the rich, satisfying pleasure and joy of God. There are two specific motivations I want to warn you of when it comes to surrender.

Beware of surrendering for the sake of your reputation. This is a common error. Growing up, I went to a summer camp several times where I fell into this trap. At the end of the week the entire camp of around a thousand people would get in line to throw a stick into a fire. This stick, we were told, symbolized our lives. We were called to throw that stick into the fire as a sign of surrendering our entire lives to God. Like cattle, almost everyone in the room took part. What was wrong was that there were many who were unwilling to surrender their hearts to the rule of King Jesus on the inside but cared much about what others thought on the outside. It was easy to get in line, start crying, grab that stick, and slowly drop it into the fire to mark yourself as one of the "surrendered ones."

Now, I do not want to bash everyone there. There really were people who were genuine. I remember times that I felt so ashamed of my unwillingness to surrender to God that I reached a breaking point at that final service. Those were times where God worked in my heart at that place. However, I am ashamed to admit, there were times when I got in line and threw a stick into the fire because I wanted my pastor to see me as a better person. The result was pretend surrender. It had nothing to do with pleasing God. It was all about me trying to gain approval and praise. Beware of this. It can be easy to look "surrendered" on the outside to promote yourself. Pretend surrender is not real surrender.

There is a second warning about false surrender. *Beware of surrendering for the sake of God owing you some kind of reward*. I am reminded of this by the attitude of the disciples at one particular point in Jesus' ministry:

> *"Then Peter said in reply, 'See, we have left everything and followed you. What then will we have?'"* (Matt. 19:27)

Peter spoke for all the disciples when he expressed this concern to Jesus. He refers to the extent of the disciples' surrender. They left everything they had and everything they were living for to follow Jesus. The problem was many of them had a wrong motivation. They were hoping for an earthly kingdom. The disciples really believed that Jesus was going to set up a kingdom in Jerusalem and finally free them from the control of the Roman government. At this point, they failed to see the spiritual victory that Jesus was accomplishing. Jesus did not come to establish an earthly victory, but instead a spiritual victory.

Peter was asking Jesus, "What's in it for us?" He believed that there was some kind of special reward for surrendering to Jesus and following Him. The disciples all thought this way. In fact, they argued often about who was going to get the biggest reward in the earthly kingdom they thought was about to begin. They wanted to be rewarded with the right hand seat next to Jesus when He became King.

Now, it can be easy to look at the disciples and think that they were just being foolish. However, if we are honest, we fall into that same trap. Many Christians surrender to God thinking that God is going to improve all of their circumstances. Jesus never promised that. All of the rewards Jesus promised for those who would follow Him were spiritual blessings. Many of those were in reference to a future kingdom after this earthly life. Do not seek earthly reward for spiritual surrender. It is a selfish motivation. It is a conditional surrender, because there is still pride ruling in the heart that seeks pleasure through selfish ambition. Beware of this in your heart.

Both of these motivations are false surrenders. When our motivations to surrender are all about our reputation improving or the rewards that we think God will owe us, we are not really surrendering everything. True surrender begins with brokenness, not selfish ambition. It gives everything to God for His pleasure instead of our pleasure or reward. God is not fooled by fake, pretend, half-hearted, conditional, or even convenient surrender. It is painful for Him. Jesus uncovered hypocrisy and false surrender all throughout His earthly ministry.

> *"You hypocrites! Well did Isaiah prophesy of you, when he said: 'This people honors me with their lips, but their heart is far from me'"* (Matt. 15:7-8).

Real surrender is not an outside act, but an inside revolution. Do not fall into a self-centered trap. Heed the warning. If you are at a place of surrender, simply ask yourself, "Why am I surrendering? What is my motivation?" We are called to surrender—to give ourselves completely away to God—because He is the rightful owner of us. He created and paid for us through Jesus' sacrifice. If you are motivated to surrender for any other reason than obedience to God out of love and worship, chances are you are being motivated to a fake surrender.

Chapter 6 Study Questions

What is fake surrender?

Describe the surrender of the Pharisee in Luke 18.

Describe the way the disciples' surrender was conditional.

What are two wrong motivations for surrender? Why are these motives wrong?

List some ways that you have been wrongly motivated to surrender.

What must be our motivation for true surrender? Why is that the only way?

7

Biblical Surrender

"So then, brothers, we are debtors, not to the flesh, to live according to the flesh. For if you live according to the flesh you will die, but if by the Spirit you put to death the deeds of the body, you will live. For all who are led by the Spirit of God are sons of God." Rom. 8:12-14

SURRENDER AND YOU

As this book comes to a close, it is only fitting that we take the concept of surrender beyond the hypothetical. So let us be specific. *Where* does your life intersect with faith and repentance? Better yet, where *should* your life intersect with faith and repentance?

Perhaps your conscience is annoying you about some area of your life, some habit, some instance of the past, some motivation for what you do, some attitude deeply embedded, some way of thinking that does not leave room for dependence on God. What are you going to do with that? If the principles we have covered apply, would you consider taking the path of surrender?

I understand that you may have read through the chapters of this book looking for errors, scrutinizing the author's writing style. You certainly have grounds to! Regardless, can you push beyond that for a moment? Can you take the basic principles discussed and allow a personal interaction with the truth presented? It may be that God has, in the faintest whisper of a way, identified something about your heart. Now is the time to be honest. Now is the time—not later.

DON'T "LET GO AND LET GOD"

In the introduction to this book, I referred to the phrase "let go and let God" in a negative light. Now that we are here, I want to explain why that phrase is not going to work for you. But, before playing hardball, here are a few positive aspects about that approach:

It identifies your powerlessness. If the issue is an addiction or a bad habit or a sinful life pattern, you simply do not have the power to defeat it on your own. If the issue is a burden or a past experience that enshrouds you in darkness, you simply do not have the power to endure—to make it to that bright and glorious "beyond."

It identifies God's power. God has the power to achieve victory for you and in you. God also has the power to carry your burdens and provide you the peace that is out of reach.

Both reasons are truthful. You are powerless, and God is all-powerful. Is that enough to radically change your life—your direction? It is certainly catchy. Are catchphrases definitive enough to address a definite issue that you are dealing with? Please do not get me wrong. I think many people have been encouraged in the right direction from catchphrases like the one mentioned based on the positives listed above. However, most of life's difficult circumstances and consequences require more definition if true change is to occur. Here are a few examples.

Bob is addicted to pornography. He has been hiding it from his wife and his friends for years. Bob is desperate for change, but every time he tries a new tactic, he is never successful. If I were to say to Bob, "just let go and let God," he might be prone to recognize some important truths: he is powerless and God is all-powerful. He is holding on to his love for pleasure and he needs to give it up. So, Bob goes home and turns his addiction over to God. But the next day Bob is faced with overwhelming urges to look at pornography. He "lets go and lets God" again. But still, the urges remain. And they remain the next day, and the next day, and again the next.

Why is Bob struggling? Why is he not free? Because the expectation in "let go and let God" is that God is going to remove the temptation. All Bob needs to do is give his struggle to God and God will do a miracle, right? Not exactly. The reason this does not help Bob in the end is because Bob is never going to get to the root of the problem. He is also never going to get to the root of the solution. He needs more definition, a more clear and direct way to address the true problem and how to respond. Bob needs to be guided through the process of faith and repentance by the clear instruction from God in

Scripture. That clear guidance will help Bob see the true state of his heart, finding the answers in what *God says* Bob needs to do.

What will Bob find in Scripture? In Jeremiah 17, Bob will find that his heart cannot be trusted. In James 5, he will find that he needs accountability. In Romans 12, he will find that he needs to present his body as a living sacrifice. In Galatians 5, he will find that he needs to walk by the Spirit. In Ephesians 6, he will find that he needs the armor of God. In Ephesians 4, he will find that he needs to starve out his sinful appetites and instead feed His mind with truth. All of that is to *follow* what Bob must do first in surrendering—repenting in faith. "Let go and let God" might be helpful in the initial direction to look to God, but it often leads people to an approach in surrender that is directionless in the long-term. In the least, it is indirect in the short-term.

Here is another example, but this one is not an issue of sin. Judy has never been the same after her miscarriage. She and her husband had tried for 10 years. All hope was lost. When she received confirmation from her doctor that she was indeed pregnant, her life was a flurry of joy and excitement. Two months later, she was pushed beyond the brink of devastation when the baby's heart stopped beating. What made her experience even more traumatic was that she had to undergo a DNC. Now, Judy's life seems to be ruled by that horrific loss. She weeps hourly. Her joy over the simple blessings in life is gone. Each new day delivers the same pain over and over again.

If I were to say to Judy in the counseling room, "you will find peace if you only let go and let God," she might be prone

BIBLICAL SURRENDER

to recognize some important truths: she is powerless to carry this heavy burden and God is powerful and able to carry it for her. She is never going to escape her pain if she carries it alone. So, Judy goes home and releases her pain to God. She cries out to Him and does feel a sense of easement. However, she cannot turn on the tv or go outside without seeing children playing or walking with a parent. That pain wrenches her soul again and again. Every time she releases it to God, she is never completely free and at peace for the long-term.

Why is Judy still overcome by her painful experience? Why can she not escape—even when she gives it to God? Because the expectation in "let go and let God" is that God is going to remove the pain. All Judy needs to do is release her pain to God and He will perform a miracle, right? Not exactly. The reason this is not really going to heal Judy in the end is because Judy is never going to get to the heart of her experience. She is also never going to get to the root of the solution. She needs more direction, a more clear and direct way to understand the God that allowed her pain, and learn how to respond to Him. Judy needs to be guided through a process that shows her *Who* this God is that she is to have faith in. That clear guidance will help Judy see the comforting realities of God's character, and will direct her to find answers in what *God says* Judy needs to do.

What will Judy find in Scripture? In Lamentations 3 and 2 Corinthians 1, Judy will find that God is not cruel. In 2 Samuel 12, she will find that there is hope to one day see her baby. In Job, she will find that God's wisdom is beyond human understanding. In James 1, she will find that suffering is allowed by God for a special purpose. All of that is to *follow* what Judy must first do in surrendering—turning to God in faith. "Let go and let God" might be helpful in the initial direction to look to God, but it does not help Judy trust that this God is *good*.

CLOSING THOUGHTS

Catchy "Christianese" is often what people turn to in dealing with life's greatest struggles, not because they intend to ignore God, but because they have not had solid direction leading them to find Him in the pages of Scripture. Biblical surrender is one of a thousand topics like that. I hope that through these basic illustrations, if anything, you can catch the importance of seeing clearly through the lens of God's words. My aim is not to belittle those who find solace in phrases like "let go and let God." Instead, I hope to illustrate through this little book that God is available, His wisdom is available, and His power is available because He made His Word available. When we take a topic like Biblical Surrender and seek to understand it using God's words, we find with a much clearer precision *how* we are to live it out.

I can think of no greater way to end this book than turning your attention to the Word of God. Surrendering to God is 1) a change of mind leading to 2) a change of heart that leads to 3) a change in action which results in 4) a changed life. God's Word shows us that we need it. God's Word shows us how He crafts it within us. God's Word shows us how to respond to it. God's Word shows us how we are to continue in it. *God's Word is the key that you and I need for a life of surrender.*

So what are you going to do with it? Will you leave the "Biblical" out of surrender and just put up a white flag, hoping God will swoop in and provide a miracle so you can continue your life? Or will you surrender in the way God prescribes it in His Word, turning to Him and hanging on His every Word as an unshakeable truth of *Who* He is and what He demands? In Biblical surrender, you will find that the storm of your life may not be removed. However, as the storm continues, you will be in a position of trusting God and seeing His transforming power at work in you.

I pray that you will be driven to true Biblical surrender after reading this book, not because the way the book describes it, but because of the God who prescribes it. Turn to Him today. Trust in Him. If you need to repent, do not wait another minute. If you need to give up the throne of your heart and submit to Him for the first time, He is ready to receive you. Whatever that "thing" is in your life, no matter how painful, controlling, or crippling, God cares deeply. He is bigger and more powerful than the hold it has on you. And He is waiting for you to turn to Him in faith. Will you surrender?

For you did not receive the spirit of slavery to fall back into fear, but you have received the Spirit of adoption as sons, by whom we cry, "Abba! Father!" (Rom. 8:15)

Chapter 7 Study Questions

Has your conscience been stirred after reading this book? If so, in what way(s)?

In what ways are phrases like "let go and let God" helpful for surrender?

How are phrases like "let go and let God" insufficient to fully guide someone who needs to surrender?

How can we get clear direction for Biblical surrender?

What are some ways that you can apply the truths discussed in this book?

www.ingramcontent.com/pod-product-compliance
Lightning Source LLC
Chambersburg PA
CBHW072208100526
44589CB00015B/2419